How to Use Temporary Help Services Effectively

A Step by Step Guide to Using Temp Agencies Services

||||||| ||| ||||||| |||| |||||||| ||| |||||
I0462869

By Meir Liraz

Published by BizMove
www.bizmove.com

ISBN: 9781090394217

Table of Contents

MEIR LIRAZ

1. Introduction

How do you cope with unexpected personnel shortages? Many businesses are facing this question whether the cause is seasonal peaking, inventory taking, special projects, several employees on sick leave at the same time, or an unexpected increase in business.

Many companies are finding a convenient and economical solution to such problems in the services of temporary personnel firms. This guide explains these services, points out some of their advantages and outlines some steps that can be taken to ensure getting the best possible results from using them.

Almost every business needs extra help at one time or another. A rush order comes in. The work load suddenly zooms and then drops back to normal when the rush order is finished. More employees than usual are absent because of illness or vacations. A special project has to have attention right away. Seasonal demands must be met or inventories must be taken without disrupting your usual business. The extra-heavy workload puts a strain on you, on your employees, and on your budget because of the overtime it requires.

These temporary shortages of personnel are especially hard for the owner-manager of the smaller businesses to handle. Their staff is small. There is little leeway for shifting schedules. Yet they cannot afford to keep on their payrolls workers who are not needed when the workload is at a normal level.

The use of temporary personnel is a relatively new approach to solving many of the personnel problems facing both large and small businesses. You can hire these extra workers by recruiting them yourself or using a private employment agency. Or you can call on a temporary personnel service firm to meet your needs. These specialized firms are usually equipped to supply you with a wide variety of people, or, in the case of some of the larger services, handle a complete department including supervisors and workers.

2. What Is A Temporary Personnel Service?

A temporary personnel service is not an employment agency. Like many service firms, it hires people as its own employees and assigns them to companies requesting assistance. This means that when you use such a service, you are not hiring an employee; you are buying the use of their time. The temporary personnel firm is responsible for payroll, bookkeeping, tax deductions, workers compensation, fringe benefits and all other similar costs connected with the employee. You are relieved of the burden of recruiting, interviewing, screening and even testing and training if these are necessary. Most national temporary personnel companies also offer performance guarantees and fidelity bonding at no added cost to their clients. In addition, you are relieved of the need for government forms and for reporting withholding tax, etc. The temporary service firm takes these responsibilities.

You may contract for a secretary, a word processing operator, a bookkeeper, a switchboard operator, a product demonstrator, a packer, added sales personnel or any of many other types of office, professional, and industrial workers. You may contract for temporary personnel for a day or for a much longer period of time.

Whatever help you need, a temporary personnel service will try to provide the right person for the job. Some temporary personnel companies specialize in one type of help, such as office workers. Others can supply a broad range of personnel from unskilled labor to accountants and engineers.

Some of the other areas where temporary personnel are profitable to use include a temporary second shift to allow you to make the most use of expensive equipment investments. Sales blitzes to introduce new products, special quarterly or year end invoicing problems, special telephone sales programs or order taking, and seasonal catalog sales are examples. Some companies contract for teams of temporary people to perform microfilming of documents, retrieval of information, and maintenance of files. Temporaries also find wide use at trade shows, product sampling or demonstrations. National temporary firms can offer the smaller company a means of handling a national marketing effort that allows them to compete with larger organizations without excessive permanent overhead.

3. Why Not Hire Your Own Temporary Personnel?

Hiring temporary workers on your own has several important disadvantages. For one thing, it may hamper your efforts to attract good permanent employees. Layoffs when an emergency has passed can lower moral among the regular employees and, if it happens too often, gives your firm a reputation for instability.

Another disadvantage is that you may not be able to get help when you need it. There may be times when the labor market is tight and the skills you need are not readily available. Also, you may feel that the time you spend in orienting new people for short-term employment is largely wasted.

The financial aspects of hiring short-term personnel is also of major importance. On the surface it may appear that using temporary personnel costs more than hiring additional employees yourself, but there are many costs that are not usually considered. As an example, mandatory costs, such as social security, unemployment insurance, workers compensation, etc., amounts to over 11% of the basic salary. Payment for time not worked including vacations, holidays and sick days, amounts to almost 9%. Then there are company paid benefits such as health insurance, pension plans, discounts and recordkeeping, payroll and other paperwork amounts to another 6-7%. Total hidden costs are in the neighborhood of 42%.

4. Advantages Of Using A Temporary Services Firm

People supplied by a temporary service firm are quickly available. Usually they can start the day after the request has been made and, in some cases, can even be made available the same day. Experienced and well qualified, they need little, if any, assistance. They usually walk in and begin functioning right away. Using people from this source, you can adjust to fast-breaking opportunities or problems without interrupting your regular production schedule.

Some companies need temporary help every week for a few hours, for example for payroll computation. Others need temporary workers for full days at various time - regularly or occasionally.

The hourly rate you pay a temporary service firm is generally higher than the base hourly or weekly salary you would pay an employee you hired yourself; however, the cost of getting the work done is less. Using a temporary services firm does away with many personnel and recordkeeping operations that are costly and time consuming. The costs of maintaining records and filing forms for fringe benefits, payroll taxes and administration are eliminated. So are the costs of advertising, screening responses, interviewing, testing, checking references and all of the other functions needed to bring a new employee into the company. In addition, you save the cost of training, of overtime and idle periods. When you use a temporary firm you pay for the actual time worked only. You do not have to pay for lunch hours, vacations, sick days and other areas of non-productivity. Every company has some department where turnover is high. By using temporary personnel for such jobs you can improve your turnover statistics .

5. When Not To Use A Temporary Service

In considering whether or not to use a temporary service, the disadvantages to your company as well as the advantages must be considered. In some cases regular employees who lose overtime pay because of the temporary workers will become a morale problem. In other cases the work may be highly specialized and require a period of training, even though it may be short. This may make the use of temporary personnel less economical.

Basically, if you need temporary personnel for a period of six months or more it is advisable to hire a full time employee. There are also cases where the job may be so complex that it requires a great deal of supervision for a worker who is unfamiliar with your way of doing things. In such instances, it may be more economical to pay overtime to a regular employee than to use a temporary worker.

6. What Will It Cost?

Charges by temporary service firms vary widely with the type of help you are contracting for. Obviously, rates will be higher for the more skilled office or industrial worker than they will be for the less skilled. Rates vary from city to city also since most temporary service firms pay their employees the going rate in that particular area for a given job. They charge you in accordance with this rate plus a basic markup that covers administrative costs plus a fair profit for the service.

You pay an hourly rate to the temporary service firm. They, in turn, pay the employee for the hours worked and take care of payroll taxes, workmen's compensation and so on.

Most reputable services do not charge you for the hours worked by an unsatisfactory worker if you let them know promptly that you are dissatisfied. Generally, you must notify them within four hours after the employee reports for work, but this provision varies with individual firms.

What you save by using temporary services depends on your individual situation. If you are to get the most for your investment, you must carefully analyze your needs and plan carefully to make the best possible use of the time and skills of the employee being supplied by the temporary service firm. The guidelines that follow will be helpful.

7. How To Select A Temporary Service Firm?

There are a great many temporary service firms throughout the country. Many are located in large population centers, some operating regionally and a few nationally. If you are likely to need temporary workers, it is a good idea to do some exploring in advance.

Check with you local Chamber of Commerce, your attorney, your accountant, your banker. Look in the yellow pages of the telephone directory under "Employment, Temporary" or "Employment Contractors - Temporary Help" or a similar heading.

Try to meet in person with the executive of the firm you select. A short discussion will help them understand your operation, problems and needs. You, in turn, can gain an understanding of just what service the company provides.

You should evaluate the company and its ability to serve you properly by most of these factors.

Reliability: Is the service a well established company with a history of success and financial stability? You might want to check their annual report if its a public company or ask for a certified financial statement to determine if they are a stable organization.

Recruiting: Competition for skilled, reliable employees in today's labor market is intense. The firm that has an aggressive recruiting program is more likely to have the most skilled and reliable employees to send you.

Testing and evaluating: What method of testing and evaluating personnel is used to assure that you will receive quality people when needed? Does the firm check references?

Training Programs: Certain skills are always in short supply regardless of employment conditions. Does the company train people in various aspects of office work, such as modern office equipment, word processing equipment, records management, upgrading of typing and shorthand skills, etc.? The company should carefully train operators on the newest types of equipment and in the newest techniques.

Retention Programs: Does the company have a good program to keep qualified employees for longer periods of time? This can assure you that you will again get qualified people when you need them in the near future.

Professional Permanent Staff: If you want to deal with knowledgeable professionals who will know and understand your needs, the temporary service firm should be staffed by people experienced in the personnel field.

Knowledge of Your Needs: Does the firm make any effort to investigate your needs and do they seem to understand what you are discussing with them as far as needs for personnel?

Prompt Service: The temporary service firm that has a supply of people available for you on short notice can be most important when you are in a rush.

Quality Control: Does the company make some effort to check back with you and determine the quality of the individual as far as they relate to your work?

Insurance Protection: Does the firm protect your company with ample insurance coverage including fidelity bonds, workers compensation, and other problems that might arise?

Guarantee: Does the temporary service firm guarantee your satisfaction with each and every temporary employee sent to you? Does it have a refund or guarantee policy? What are its terms?

8. Plan Early

The key to the successful use of temporary employees is in planning what type of help you will need, how much and when. The amount of accurate information you give to the temporary service firm will determine the efficiency they will have in supplying the correct people for your needs.

To plan properly for the use of a temporary service you must answer these questions:

How seasonal is my business?

Do any of my regular employees have to work overtime to meet peak workloads? If so, what does the overtime cost?

If any extensive amount of overtime is needed, will there be a performance lag and possible morale problems during regular working hours?

With better planning could I spread out any of the peak work loads through the year?

Are my deliveries made on schedule?

Do customers often come up with rush jobs?

If so, can I get them to plan their needs further in

advance?

Are my employees' vacations scheduled not to interfere with peak seasons?

What extra help do I need to cope with these problems and reduce costs?

Plan discussion sessions with key personnel, those involved with planning day to day operations. Study your production schedule. Note peak periods. Compare this year with previous years. A pattern will begin to emerge and you will be able to see where some extra help would have avoided problems and kept your costs down. Many temporary service firms will supply trained personnel to advise you in this regard.

9. What to Do When The Time Comes

If it is decided that you can use temporary help, it is extremely important that you inform them of exactly what is needed. A good temporary firm will have detailed description forms about your company and the positions you are filling with their services so that they can furnish the proper employee for you. They will ask for information such as the department they will be working in, the duration of the assignment, your working hours, your dress code, smoking rules, and other information that is important for the service to know. Will you be needing a copy typist or a clerk-typist for example? Does the secretarial position require shorthand or are there machine transcriptions to do? What type of software and office equipment are involved? Are there any special knowledges or skills needed? You will find that by informing the service of your exact needs you will have qualified people furnished to you and will not be paying for skills that are not needed for your individual assignment. Most of the larger temporary service firms have special advisors who will work with you and help you plan ahead. In summary:

Estimate your needs

Decide what the specific requirements of the job are. Exactly what talents do you need? How long will you need the employee?

Don't ask for someone with higher qualifications than the work calls for or the cost will be unnecessarily high. On the other hand, don't try to economize by getting under-qualified help and then expecting the worker to carry out tasks that he or she isn't prepared to handle.

Give the temporary-help service full information

If the temporary personnel firm is to help you get the best results at the lowest possible cost, you must give its people detailed information about the work to be done. Tell them the nature of your business, the working hours, when and how long you'll need help, the skills required, the types of equipment to be operated. You may want to send samples of the work to be done, if it is feasible. Be sure to give the exact location of your business, transportation available, parking information, and the name and

title of the person to whom the temporary
employee is to report.

10. Preparing For The Temporary Employee

A few steps taken before the temporary employee reports for work will do much to make the association a success, both for the employee and for you.

ONE - Arrange for supervision

Appoint one of your permanent employees to supervise the temporary employee and check on the progress of the work from time to time. Be sure this supervisor understands the job to be done and just what his or her own responsibility is.

TWO - Tell your permanent employees

It's a good idea to let your staff know that you are taking on extra help and that it will be temporary. Explain why the extra help is needed and ask them to cooperate with the new employee in any way possible.

THREE - Prepare the physical facilities

Have everything ready before the temporary worker arrives. The work to be done should be organized and laid out so that the employee can begin producing with a minimum of time spent in adjusting to the job and the surrounding. See that the materials needed are available and the equipment is in place and in good working order.

FOUR - Plan the work load

Don't set up schedules that are impossible to complete within the time you allot. Try to stay within the time limits you gave the temporary-help service, but plan to extend the time period, if necessary, rather than crowd the employee. Rushing and overwork can result in costly mistakes.

FIVE - Prepare detailed instructions

Describe your type of business, the products you manufacture or the services you offer. Be specific in outlining the procedures your company follows. Most employees of temporary-help services adjust quickly to the methods of an individual firm because of their varied experience.

11. The Work Begins

You've made all the preparations. The employee has arrived and is ready to start work. What now? How do you get a temporary worker started? What should you expect? What if you're not satisfied?

This is the crucial stage of the relation between your company and the temporary employee. Get off to a good start and the rest will go smoothly.

ONE - Help the employee settle in

Receive the temporary employee as you would receive one hired on a permanent basis. Make the person feel like a member of your team. Explain where to hang coats, the location of the washroom, the lunch hour, coffee breaks, and so on.

Introduce the temporary employee to the permanent employee who will supervise the work.

Introduce the temporary employee also to permanent employees in the same department. Explain that "Ms. Jones will be here for a few days to help out". Or, "Mr. Smith will be here this week to help get out the rush job."

TWO - Explain the job

Go over the work assignment and the instructions. Explain company routines. Make your directions as simple as possible and provide samples of the work to be done. If the work is complex, explain it clearly and make certain that your explanation is understood. Assure the temporary employee of your staff's cooperation and willingness to help, and show your own interest and concern.

THREE - Don't expect the impossible

How much can you expect from a temporary employee? Fully as much as you contracted for with the service firm. Most employees of temporary personnel firms perform well. They are experienced and versatile. Because they have worked for a variety of businesses, they have learned to adapt quickly to a new situation, and they know that future assignments depend on their doing satisfactory work.

But don't expect the impossible. Don't overload temporary employees - make a slight allowance for the fact that they are not familiar with your business and its operations. Check the work occasionally, ask for any questions, never leave the employee feeling stranded or left out. At the same time, don't make them nervous by hovering over them. And don't push or prod too much.

12. Judging The Overall Results

Within a few hours after the temporary worker has reported, you will be able to judge how the work is going. If you are not satisfied, you should not hesitate to call the temporary service firm and inform them of the problems. Most reliable temporary service firms will call you to see how the person is working out and take corrective action if required.

A good temporary service firm will ask you to evaluate the employee's work at the end of the assignment.

You have a right to expect a conscientious, interested employee who will put in a full day's work.

You should also judge the use of temporary services in your business operation. To do this, you should keep these points in mind to help you plan for future needs:

Did the productivity of the employee justify the cost? Was the work completed accurately and effectively?

Did it benefit the impact on your overall

operations? Were there any disadvantages?

After you have evaluated the above points, you can consult with your key people and the temporary service firm to evaluate your needs for the future. You may be able to work out a program for hiring temporary personnel throughout the year so that you will be fully covered for workloads at all times.